How not 2 Hate Your Job

13 ViewPoints For Satisfaction At Work

Eric M. Watterson

How NOT 2 Hate Your Job:
13 Viewpoints For Satisfaction At Work
by Eric M. Watterson

CENTRY™ Curriculum
© 2018 All rights reserved.
ISBN: 978-1-718-69594-8
Visit Us Online at: CENTRY.me

Printed in the United States of America. All rights reserved. No part of this book may be reproduced in whole or in part in any form without the express written consent of the publisher.

Why I Wrote This Book & How It Will Help?

Just like a lot of other people, I've worked several different jobs in my life. Some I enjoyed while others, not so much. I've worked as a cashier, computer lab tech, parking lot attendant, factory line worker, store manager, graphic designer and video editor just to name a few. All of this despite my ultimate desire of making movies, creating content and helping people, even though I had no idea how to get there. I understand that each job I've had, has been part of my path towards finding my ultimate purpose in life. However, no matter what job I've had, I've been able to appreciate it for what it was with a good attitude, while working towards other goals.

However, a lot of people seem to suffer on their jobs as if their jobs are their life's purpose. Unfortunately, many people in our society label others based on the jobs they have, the cars they drive or the money they make with no idea of the potential that people carry within them for greatness.

I wrote this book in hopes to connect with those people that may be like me that have worked jobs that weren't fulfilling their truest desires. However, with the proper mindset, they can learn to appreciate their job for what it is and use it as fuel towards their future.

With the right perspective, people don't have to hate their jobs and I want this information to help them. If this is you, these 13 keys are designed to help you NOT Hate Your Job!

My sincere desire is that this book and everything else I write, create and produce will have a positive and inspiring impact on families, relationships and individuals.

To Your Success,

Eric M. Watterson

TABLE OF CONTENTS

THE CONDITION 7
THE NEED 11
THE VIEWPOINTS 17
#1 UNDERSTAND IT 19
#2 APPRECIATE THE FACT 21
#3 MAKE THE MOST 25
#4 ACCEPT YOUR VALUE 29
#5 AVOID THE GOSSIP 33
#6 DON'T COMPLAIN 37
#7 KNOW YOUR IMPORTANCE 41
#8 FIND THE PURPOSE 45
#9 STRIVE FOR EXCELLENCE 49
#10 MAKE IT ABOUT OTHERS 53
#11 BRING THE SUNSHINE 55
#12 BECOME POSITIVELY NOTICEABLE 57
#13 EVERYTHING MATTERS 61
MY BOSS IS A JERK 65
    UNDERSTAND THE POSITION 66
    UNDERSTAND THE PERSON 67
    UNDERSTAND THE TIME 69
    UNDERSTAND THE CONTROL 70
AFTER WORK 73
    PURSUE HAPPINESS 75
    PURSUE PURPOSE 76
THINGS TO CONSIDER 79
CLOSING 81
BIBLIOGRAPHY 83
OTHER BOOKS 85
FOLLOW US @ 87
MORE INFO 89

THE CONDITION

con·di·tion [kuh n-dish-uh n] noun – a particular mode of being of a person or thing; existing state; situation with respect to circumstances.

The unemployment rate is determined by the share of the labor force currently without a job but seeking employment. In 2016, the civilian labor force of the United States numbered 159.19 million. There are a number of reasons why people may not be currently working. Some by choice, like early retirement, while others aren't chosen, such as illness, caring for others, company downsizing, layoffs or lack of opportunities, just to name a few. There's also a growing concern for individuals who have been unemployed so long they lose hope or the desire to continue searching for a job.[1] However, despite all of this, there are still a lot of people working jobs faithfully and making ends meet.

> *"The world is full of willing people, some willing to work, the rest willing to let them."*
> ~ Robert Frost

So, no matter how bad it may feel, if you have a job, you have something to be grateful for. It may not be exactly what you want, and it may not be perfect; however, it could be worse.

With that said, if you're reading this, we can come to one of the following basic conclusions:
- You currently have a job, or you're confident that you'll get another one soon;
- You're at a job you need, but you're not happy;
- You're doing all you can, or know to do to maintain your job;
- You know of people or situations that are worse than yours, or;
- You hate your job and you're reading this to see if it could help.

"It's a recession when your neighbor loses his job; it's a depression when you lose yours."
~ Harry S Truman

The point then becomes:
- How do I not hate this job that I know I need?

- How do I not hate this job that someone else wishes they had?
- How can I get to a point where I'm doing my best during the hours that I am at work?

So, let's discuss some simple concepts and truths that we believe will help you.

13 Viewpoints For Satisfaction At Work

THE NEED

need [need] noun – a requirement, necessary duty, or obligation; a lack of something wanted or deemed necessary; necessity arising from the circumstances of a situation or case:

We live in a society where, quite frankly, we all need a job or to be a part of an organization that works towards a goal to gain income and hopefully advance the lives of others. There are some people that desire not to live under those conditions, but we are not talking about them. So most of us, work for a company as an employee to produce income and better ourselves and our society. People go to their different jobs, in their different industries to meet the different needs of our society. So, let's talk briefly about these levels and instead of starting at the bottom and going up, let's start at the top and go down as we discuss these levels.

The highest goal of a job is, again, to advance us as a society in some way. America is a blessed country. However, whether you are an American or not, the advancement of whatever country or nation you live in is the culmination of every citizen doing their part and interacting in relationship and business.

> *"Normal is getting dressed in clothes that you buy for work and driving through traffic in a car that you are still paying for - in order to get to the job you need to pay for the clothes and the car, and the house you leave vacant all day so you can afford to live in it." ~ Ellen Goodman*

Drop down a level to your individual state or city and consider that your city has hundreds of businesses that help feed the economy where you live. The more people interact and provide services, the more your city can provide for its residents. Every city has a responsibility to do what it can to help its residents and businesses enhance the economy to provide for its citizens.

From there, let's consider the individual companies, both large and small. Each company needs workers to help it fulfill a need. For example, your phone company needs people to help it fulfill its goal of providing phone service. Within the company, they will need a person or persons to complete certain tasks for the company to successfully provide phone service to its target market.

For example:
- Someone is needed to calculate the price of the phone service the company will provide;
- Someone is needed to market the services of the company;
- Someone is needed to take the orders for new service:
- Someone is needed to process the credit cards, checks or cash for the service;
- Someone is needed to schedule appointments for the installation of the service;
- Someone is needed to visit homes and install the equipment for the service;
- Someone is needed to provide customer service and billing; and,
- Someone is needed to send invoices for the actual service itself.

These different "Someones" are examples of the people required for the company to meet their targeted need in society, keep the cycle going and make a profit. Hopefully not so much of a profit that it's highway robbery, but a profit none-the-less.

Finally, the last level we'll look at is the one closest to home which is the individual employee or worker that has to:
- Use an alarm to wake up but feels like they just went to sleep;
- Wake up the kids, and get them off to school;
- Fight through traffic that's always moving slower then normal;
- Clock in, grab coffee and open emails;
- Say "good morning" to other people who are barely awake;
- Take lunch and break around people and conversations they don't understand;
- Respect a boss they think is from another planet;
- Ignore loud conversations that their coworkers have with their mom, children or girlfriends;
- Try not to stare at the clock during board meetings;
- Stand in line behind the new guy that still doesn't know how to clock out;

- Get back in traffic with 10,000 people going the exact same way they are;
- Pickup the kids, walk the dog, help the kids do homework, make dinner and prepare them for bed;
- All of this just to do it again the next day.

Now, of course all of these items won't apply to every person, but this is just an example of what a lot of people may need to deal with on an average day. The point is, every level fits together as part of a greater whole. Sometimes, it's hard to see the really big picture and where we fit in it because of all the individual pieces that make up our individual days and lives.

We want to help you see how you fit in the big picture and on your job, so that as things happen throughout your day, they don't cause you to lose sight of how important you are to your job, and the purpose it serves in your life. We want you to grow to appreciate your time on your job and see how you contribute to it as an employee and how you impact society as a whole.

THE VIEWPOINTS

view·point [vyoo-point] noun – a place affording a view of something; position of observation: an attitude of mind: a perspective specific to position

Our perceptions create our realities. To each one of us, our minds, or our ways of thinking, would be the first thing we would need to change on the road towards not hating our jobs. We, as human beings, create concepts in our minds and act on them whether they are true or not.

We've all seen those people on the American Idol auditions that stand in line for days because they "know" they can sing. To them, they have been given a gift to sing, without which, the whole world is suffering. The harsh reality is that they really need true friends! A true friend would have told some of them NOT to go on American Idol because they quite frankly just CAN'T sing! The fact that some people need friends that will help them adjust their distorted viewpoints is a topic we'll discuss another time.

However, for the time being let's talk about a few viewpoints that will help us appreciate the jobs we have.

#1

UNDERSTAND IT

What you don't understand, you'll take advantage of, mistreat and underestimate.

un-der-stand-ing [uhn-der-stan-ding] noun – mental process used when a person who comprehends; comprehension; personal interpretation; intellectual faculties; intelligence; mind:

Your job is part of your life. It's a vital part of how you do what you do, and it should be appreciated. However, it's important to understand where your job fits into your life, but it's not necessarily the purpose of your life. Learn to view your job as a source of income and advancement toward helping other areas of your life. If you have children, it helps you provide for them and give them a secure future. If you're a husband, it helps add value to your wife's life. As a wife, it adds value to your husband's life.

If you're single, it will help you get those clothes you need to be appealing on that next date.

In essence, your job helps your future and helps provide for the things you want in life. Just don't blow your money on sneakers, when you should be putting a little into a savings account or money market fund. Whether or not you are wise with your money, understand that your job is part of what helps you in your future.

> *"Emergencies have always been necessary to progress. It was darkness which produced the lamp. It was fog that produced the compass. It was hunger that drove us to exploration. And it took a depression to teach us the real value of a job." ~ Victor Hugo*

#2

APPRECIATE IT

It's nearly impossible to honor and value what you don't appreciate.

ap·pre·ci·ate [uh-pree-shee-eyt] verb – to be grateful or thankful for: to have gratitude for.

Being grateful in life helps you maintain a good perspective and it keeps your heart open to new possibilities. This type of viewpoint keeps your life and heart open to seeing and experiencing greater possibilities. Sometimes, we can get caught up in our own worlds and can't see the concerns of others because our own concerns are so prevalent in our minds. However, a grateful outlook helps us to stay appreciative for what we have without thinking too highly of ourselves at the same time.

"Opportunity is missed by most people because it is dressed in overalls and looks like work."
~ Thomas A. Edison

A very simple fact to keep in mind is, there are many people without clothes, without food, without shelter and without a job. Like it or not, no matter how mad your Cheese-Head Boss makes you, at least you have a job where you have to deal with a Cheese-Head Boss in the first place. Think about it this way, which would you prefer, to stand in the unemployment line with your Cheese-Head Boss or deal with them from 9 to 5?

Take the time to focus on what you have, and what life would be like without it. To take it a little further, think about not just your life but think of the lives of those that count on you and need you in their life to make it. Where would they be without you? Appreciation first begins with realizing what you have, and the realization that there is someone, somewhere that does not have what you have and may need it just as badly, if not worse than you. This other person, if they had what you have, may be much more appreciative than you.

Make a conscious effort to be grateful and appreciative for what you have, whether it's perfect or not doesn't matter. There's nothing about you that makes you any better than the other person that does not have what you have. At the basic level of every person we are all the same. The color of our skin is a result of the different levels of pigment; however, we all bleed the color red. The area you live in may be nicer, yet we all breathe the same oxygen. Moreover, the sun shines on everyone the same way and if there's a cloud blocking it today, just wait for the sun to come out tomorrow. No one person is better than the next. God loves us all equally. The only thing that makes us different is the quality of the decisions we make.

> *"For He maketh His sun to rise on the evil and on the good, and sendeth rain on the just and on the unjust. ~ Matthew 5:45 (The Bible)*

13 Viewpoints For Satisfaction At Work

#3

MAKE THE MOST OF IT

You must make the most of what you have, to get the most out of it.

most [mohst] adjective – in the greatest quantity, amount, measure, degree, or number; in the majority of instances; greatest, as in size or extent:

Make the most of your hours at work; be productive and busy, don't goof off. A person that goofs off is, quite frankly, a "goof." If you focus on working consistently during your work hours, you can, most likely, have your work done by five o'clock, which then can hopefully give you the freedom to leave work on time, not because you're watching the clock, but because you put in a good and full day of work. Let's be honest, most of us want to leave when the day is over, but don't want to be put into the category of an employee that watches the clock.

This is where personal integrity falls into place. If you know you worked consistently during the day, took your proper and allotted breaks and lunch time, focused on getting your assignments for the day completed properly, leaving at five o'clock shouldn't be a problem for your boss. It's the people that spend most of the day doing things other than work that need to be concerned about who's watching them leave at five o'clock. They know their work isn't done because they didn't give it the proper attention it needed. So, be honest about the work you do and how much true effort you put into it.

> *"It is not the hours we put in on the job, it is what we put into the hours that counts."*
> *~ Sidney Madwed*

If you give 50% effort into the work you do, you will only feel a 50% sense of accomplishment. Hard and consistent work will help to breed in you a sense of accomplishment and satisfaction that you'll never experience if you make a habit of being a slacker day in and day out. If you are the kind of employee that people have to stand over to get the job done, they may not think you are worth their time. A good company can find a person that takes pride in themselves and takes pride in the work they provide to their employer. Make the most of your time at work, for yourself, and the company that is paying you to do a specific job for them.

13 Viewpoints For Satisfaction At Work

#4

ACCEPT YOUR VALUE

**The true value of a thing
is often over or under evaluated.**

val·ue [val-yoo] noun – relative worth, merit, or importance; monetary or material worth, as in commerce or trade:

I don't know of any company that's willing to pay someone to do a job as a favor to them, because then they would just be throwing money away. A working relationship goes both ways. A company needs workers to help them fulfill its goal of servicing their clients and customers. While the employees give of their time, energy, training and talents to receive money in return. The money that you make is not just green paper with pictures of president's faces on it. Money represents you. It stands for your time, your energy, your ability and gifts. Money is a natural representation of you and your spiritual essence.

After you have given of your spiritual essence in time, talents and gifts, you receive payment, money or income in return. This is one reason why money is so important. It's a natural representation of who you are and how you have applied and used the essence of who God has made you to be to benefit others and humanity.

> *"People forget how fast you did a job, but they remember how well you did it."*
> *~ Howard Newton*

You are so important to your company that they are willing to pay you for the essence of who you are and what you provide. Your essence is translated into the work you do to help them achieve their mission. Don't see yourself as just another face in the crowd or another head with a number attached to it. There is something that would not get done without "you" to do it. Accept the fact that you are needed and valuable or they wouldn't pay you. Once you accept the fact that you are a valuable part of the company you work for, you will find a sense of pride rise up within you to help you fulfill whatever part that is.

Accepting your value is a personal decision and viewpoint that will stand no matter how others see and treat you. If you take a $100 Dollar Bill and ball it up, throw it in the street, mistreat it and disown it, its still a $100 Dollar Bill! All it needs is someone to recognize what it is and treat it in a way that recognizes its true value. You have value and you're important. Know the value of who you are because God made you in His image and His likeness and whoever doesn't understand or see that may not be able to see it until you do.

13 Viewpoints For Satisfaction At Work

#5

AVOID THE GOSSIP

If you don't have something good to say, don't say nothing at all!

gossip [gos-uh p] noun – idle talk or rumor, especially about the personal or private affairs of others; tattling or idle talk; to talk idly, especially about the affairs of others; go about tattling.

Gossip is considered juicy to some, but its not beneficial to hear or to participate in. For those that hear it, it will most likely give you a negative impression on others. For those that share it, it creates a negative view of you. As the old saying goes, "If they talk about someone else to you, they will talk about you to someone else."

Another reason to avoid gossip is because of the effect of the "**<u>Spontaneous Trait Transference Phenomenon</u>**". This subconscious phenomenon occurs when communicators are perceived as possessing the very traits they describe in others. Studies done on how people are viewed when they speak about others confirmed that the people speaking become associated with the traits they describe in others and those "perceived" traits persist over time. They also indicate that the spontaneous trait transference phenomenon occurs even when there are no logical bases for associating the person with the traits they describe in others. [2] So in essence, whenever you say something positive about another person, those positive traits are applied to you subconsciously by the one listening to you. On the other hand, when you say something negative about another person, those negative traits are applied to you subconsciously by the one listening to you.

Even when the gossip is true, there's a lot of truth that shouldn't be passed around. By passing around negative gossip that may be true, people by their words, create negative ways people are viewed and possibly treated. When this type of atmosphere is created, a sense of distrust is created and makes for an uncomfortable work atmosphere.

"Gossip is saying behind their back what you would not say to their face. Flattery is saying to their face what you would not say behind their back." ~ Unknown

Only childish and narrow-minded people gossip. They talk about people to purposely spread negative rumors or perspectives that may or may not be true. By purposely avoiding gossip, you avoid the people and the conversations that create a negative mindset in you and others. You have enough to be concerned about at work to do your job well and to advance the purpose of your company, so don't fill your mind and heart with gossip that will make it that much harder to work with your coworkers.

"Gossip is when you hear something you like about someone you don't." ~ Unknown

13 Viewpoints For Satisfaction At Work

#6

DON'T COMPLAIN

**Complaining is always easy,
but rarely beneficial.**

complain [kuh m-pleyn] verb – to express dissatisfaction, pain, uneasiness, censure, resentment, or grief; find fault: to tell of one's pains, ailments, etc.: to make a formal accusation:

One good way to make the most of your time at work is to watch the negative words you speak. One of the main ways we use negative words is through complaining. The problem with complaining is that if you voice a dislike without receiving a resolution, there's no beneficial outcome. If we spend our time complaining and there's no beneficial outcome from it, what good is it?

Most of the time when people complain, they're simply stating negative facts or situations to people that aren't in a position to change them or make them better. So, in these cases, what benefit is it to complain? For example, if you complain to the girl at the coffee shop about your boss, there's probably nothing she can do to make the situation better. However, if you're searching for solutions, by discussing your situation with the coffee shop girl, you may find some beneficial counsel and support because you're looking for solutions and not just searching for an opportunity to complain or someone to listen to you.

> *"Be grateful for what you have and stop complaining - it bores everybody else, does you no good, and doesn't solve any problems."*
> *~ Zig Ziglar*

When you complain, you point out the negative to other people and make their day less pleasant. The more you make their day less pleasant by pointing out the negative, the more your day becomes less pleasant by thinking and speaking about the negative. Your complaining has the potential of ruining your day and the day of someone else.

However, most complaints are based in situations and circumstances that need to be addressed and possibly changed. How much more beneficial is it to focus on solutions through communication and discussions instead of pointing out the negative by complaining and griping? So don't complain. If you don't have nothing good to say, shut up and say nothing instead of pointing out the negative to someone else.

And if you really wanna shake things up, spark up conversations that search for solutions to problems and concerns, instead of just complaining about the people and circumstances that create them. The mature person searches for solutions that the immature person just complains about.

> *"There are times in life when, instead of complaining, you do something about your complaints." ~ Rita Dove*

13 Viewpoints For Satisfaction At Work

#7

KNOW YOUR IMPORTANCE

You're important just the way you are; if you don't know it, how will anyone else?

Know [noh] verb — to perceive or understand as fact or truth; to apprehend clearly and with certainty:

Another very important part of learning how not to hate your job is knowing that what you do on your job is important. Take pride in what you do and see how it affects the entire mission and effectiveness of the company. Let's say you're a secretary and you answer calls for your boss, write memos, take notes and organize meetings. Whether you know it or not, this is a very important part of the piece that your boss is supposed to play. If you didn't help him organize and keep things in line, could he do it and make the meetings, have a clear head to make the decisions necessary? Probably not.

> *"It is difficult to get a man to understand something when his job depends on not understanding it."* ~ *Upton Sinclair*

Even if your boss is a jerk, how much more of a jerk would they be if you weren't there to take some of the pressure off of their jerkology, or jerkiness? And yes, *"jerkology"* is a real word; I made it up myself. It's described as, *"the art of being a jerk."*, and some people are really good at it! I submitted it to the folks at Webster for their dictionary, but they won't return my calls. Go figure! Anyway, sometimes we have to know our own importance, even if those around us are too self-absorbed to recognize it and thank us for what we do.

Ok, let's say you mop the floor. What would the floor look like if you weren't there to keep it clean? People who throw trash on the ground are very selfish and inconsiderate of others. No matter whether you throw trash directly on the ground or out the window of your car while driving, it always affects someone else. Someone else will have to pick it up. Someone else will step on it, or someone else will just have to look at your selfish act of not walking your lazy tail to a trash can to dispose of your own garbage properly!

> *"The test for whether or not you can hold a job should not be the arrangement of your chromosomes." ~ Bella Abzug*

If you are mopping the floors, you are helping maintain a level of pride that everyone recognizes, either consciously or unconsciously. It's one of those important things that most people only recognize when it's NOT done properly. For example, very few people notice a clean floor, but everyone notices a dirty one. Every maintenance person helps the overall morale of a company on a level that really subconsciously affects everyone positively, when they do their job well.

Take note of a hotel room. When you walk into a clean hotel room and the bed is made up, trash is emptied, and the mirrors are clean, you feel a sense of appreciation and gratitude that may never rise to your conscious mind to say "thank you" for. However, if you walk into a hotel room that is dirty, with the beds unmade and trash on the floor, and no toilet paper in the bathroom, you feel disgusted and upset. That feeling would probably make you request another room or leave the hotel altogether. The term, "cleanliness is next to godliness," is expressed in how good you feel when someone has provided you with a clean area to reside in.

No matter what your job is, you are important to that company being effective in its overall mission or goal. If you don't know the overall impact your job plays in the success of the company…ask. Have your boss explain to you why what you do is important and how it helps the company be successful. Once you truly understand your part, it will help you to take pride in the part you play. It will also make your boss notice that you want to be educated in how you are helping the company. Instantly, it will help them see value in you, because you take value in yourself and what you provide to the organization.

#8

FIND THE PURPOSE

The purpose of a thing is often found in how it's used to benefit someone else.

pur·pose [pur-puh s] noun – the reason for which something exists or is done, made, used, etc; an intended or desired result; end; aim; goal.

Everyone needs to feel appreciated. It helps us maintain a sense of well-being and gives us the energy needed to continue to strive to do better. However, there are times when we need to find our own purpose, or our own appreciation.

Unfortunately, some bosses don't know how to make a person feel appreciated. They don't know how to instill within the people under them the motivation needed to help them do their job. They fail to help their employees feel appreciated and important to the people they serve and work with.

The problem with this is that some people find importance in making other people feel unimportant. So, if you wait for someone else to help you feel important, you may never feel it. You need to be strong and confident enough in what you do to find importance and purpose for yourself.

> *"The people who are doing the work are the moving force behind the Macintosh. My job is to create a space for them, to clear out the rest of the organization and keep it at bay." ~ Steve Jobs*

So then, the next logical question is, how do you find importance in what you do? If the people and/or situations at work do not give you a sense of importance and purpose, how do you find it? One of the main things you'll need is to be able to see and understand your importance to the company. This can be hard to see if your viewpoint is filled with competition, gossip and people pleasing. Instead of complaining about your job, take the time to see how what you do affects those around you and the effectiveness of the company. It may take a little effort, but it begins with the ability to not complain about where you are, but appreciate it, which can then lead you to finding the purpose that you fill on your job.

If you strive to find purpose in what you do, you will then find a new sense of pride in doing it. This purpose will also extend beyond you to someone else. Purpose is always inclusive of someone else. So, as you search for the true purpose of what you are doing, keep looking until it includes someone else. Once what you do is not just about you, you are realizing the true value you bring to the table.

13 Viewpoints For Satisfaction At Work

#9

STRIVE FOR EXCELLENCE

**Strive for internal excellence
and others will see external excellence.**

ex·cel·lence [ek-suh-luh ns] – noun the fact or state of excelling; superiority; eminence: an excellent quality or feature:

Excellence is one of those words used often but isn't easy to define. It's one of those things that's only available when you're truly mature enough to honestly judge yourself. If you truly desire to have a standard within yourself that reaches for your personal best, you'll strive for excellence in what you do. Excellence can only really be measured from within. When "You Know" you've done your best, when people disagree with how you do your work, you have the internal pride to stand up and defend your work, or performance, because you know, within yourself, that you've given it your all.

I once had a supervisor tell me that a project I completed wasn't my best. I immediately corrected them and said, "I always do my best on every project because it's 'my personal standard'. Now, if you aren't pleased with the result of the project, then there's an expectation you have that I may not understand but need to work towards. However, my personal best and excellence is within me and NOT based on you or anyone else." Your excellence must be a standard within you that you consistently judge yourself by so even when others don't agree, you can stand by what you do because you know within yourself that it was your best.

> *"Every job is a self-portrait of the person who did it. Autograph your work with excellence."*
> *~ Commitment To Excellence*

When I ran track in school, I didn't win every race. I only really got upset with myself when I lost a race I had not tried my hardest to win. I personally have had people question my work, at times. However, my own personal belief and work ethic have always given me the stance that in everything I do, I do as an honor to God and out of respect for those that are trusting me to do my job. It always puts me in the position to not accept another person's judgment, that I have not done my best at the work I provide. Let's address why they may not like what I have done. They may have wanted it done differently. In other words, it wasn't from the stance that I didn't do my best; it was just that they may have expected something different.

As you do your work, always strive for excellence and do your best at all times. People see excellence and know when people are truly doing their best, not because the work is so good, but because they believe in the work they do. So, make everything you do on your job a noticeable expression of your personal excellence.

13 Viewpoints For Satisfaction At Work

#10

MAKE IT ABOUT OTHERS

When you do things for the benefit of others, others will do things for the benefit of you.

oth·ers [uhth -ers] pronoun – Usually, others. other persons or things; some person or thing else:

Our jobs are the things we do that affect someone or something else in some way, some shape or some form. Because you do something that affects someone or something else, you are paid for it. So in essence, you have a job because you are needed to affect someone else, so much so that people pay you for the value of your contribution to the overall effect of the company. No matter what position you have or even what your pay scale is, make what you do about the people that you work with, the customers that your company services, the products that it makes, the services that it provides.

"If you do a good job for others, you heal yourself at the same time, because a dose of joy is a spiritual cure." ~ Dietrich Bonhoeffer

Fortune Magazine once rated Google as one of the 100 best companies to work for [3] and it's not just because of how Google impacts the world; it's also about how Google impacts its employees. This internal concern that Google has for its employees helps them take pride in their work, which, in turn, affects the world. So, make an effort to find out how what you do affects others. Make that one of the driving forces that helps you not to hate, but appreciate, your job and strive for excellence in all that you do.

#11

BRING THE SUN

When You Brighten Someone Else's Day, You become Someone Others Enjoy

Sunshine [suhn-shahyn] noun – the shining of the sun; direct light of the sun; cheerfulness or happiness; a source of cheer or happiness.

There are always times that we will be down or just not have a good day. We all have them. But how great is it when you've had that bad day, and someone just says something random and nice to just bring a smile to your face just when you needed it. It doesn't necessarily take a lot of work or effort, just the desire to bring a smile to someone else and brighten their day.

> *No act of kindness, no matter how small, is ever wasted. ~ Aesop*

Sometimes we can't see the sun because of the clouds over our heads. Its at these times that we may not be able to see the sun, unless someone else brings us the sunshine in their life and shares it with us. Be that person that brings the sun into someone else's life. The more you do that, the more your own day becomes brighter simply because you desire to brighten someone else's day.

What you do for others, will then be done for you. When you desire to make someone else happy, that happiness you desire for them, becomes that much more available to you.

> *Goodness is about character - integrity, honesty, kindness, generosity, moral courage, and the like. More than anything else, it is about how we treat other people. ~ Dennis Prager*

#12

BECOME POSITIVELY NOTICEABLE

People are going to notice something about you, so make it something positive.

no·tice·a·ble [noh-ti-suh-buh l] adjective – attracting notice or attention; capable of being noticed; worthy or deserving of notice or attention; noteworthy:

We all know those people at work that you just hate to see coming down the hall. They don't speak. They don't smile. They always have a problem. They always complain. There's always something wrong with someone or something. They just don't have a positive impact on your work day or on the working environment. These are people that are, without a question, noticeable, but they are not "positively" noticeable.

They're the people that when you hear they're out from work, you're glad because they won't be there to bring down the atmosphere. When they're gone, the entire workplace is more enjoyable. It just seems like the walk to the bathroom is more pleasant because there isn't the possibility of running into them in the hall. Don't be one of them. Be a person that your co-workers enjoy.

If you don't have a positive impact on the people you work with and you desire to, here are a few steps you can take to become more positively noticeable:

1. <u>Admit it:</u> If you wouldn't like to see you coming down the hall, odds are someone else feels that way about you to. Don't lie to yourself about it. If you're a jerk and always negative you know it, so just admit it.
2. <u>Bring Gifts:</u> Bring a small gesture of kindness to others. Buy a box of donuts for all your co-workers. Donuts make people fatter, but they also bring smiles.
3. <u>Apologize:</u> By openly apologizing for the negative impact you've had on others you can open the door for new relationships.

4. <u>Get Input:</u> Sometimes it's hard to truly see ourselves and how we can be better. Asking for input helps you to see what others see. Remember it's only input. Not the law or even the truth. Just another person's perspective.
5. <u>Listen:</u> It's not easy to open yourself up to hear things that you could do better but doing so expresses maturity and can have a great impact on others. Listen with an open heart without being too hard on yourself.
6. <u>Change:</u> Change isn't always easy and takes strength. However, if you really want to change, be open to the advice of others and then put it into practice.

If your presence is making someone else's day dreadful, your day is dreadful as well. If other people don't want to talk to you because of how you act, you will not want to talk to them because of how they feel about you. It's those people that we enjoy seeing in the hall that give us a special spark of social kindness and interaction during our day. They make our time at work more enjoyable. Because they are happy and smile, they give us a piece of their joy.

Keep in mind that you can't give someone something you don't have.

> *"If you're happy in what you're doing, you'll like yourself, you'll have inner peace. And if you have that, along with physical health, you will have had more success than you could possibly have imagined." ~ Johnny Carson*

So, become a person that people enjoy seeing and miss when they are gone. If you are out sick, do people care and ask how you are doing when you return, or do they suggest you go back to the doctor because you still look a little green around the edges? When you become positively noticeable, the positive effect you have on people will make being at work a lot more fun, for you and the people you interact with on a daily basis.

#13

EVERYTHING MATTERS

If you think nothing you do matters, you're missing all of the ways in which you matter.

eve·ry·thing [ev-ree-thing] pronoun – every thing or particular of an aggregate or total; all.

So, we've talked about a few different concepts and viewpoints that will help you not to hate your job, but it's important to know that a combined focus is truly needed. As humans we are complexed beings. It's the love we show others, along with our need to be loved by others, that works together to help us truly experience a complete and fulfilling life. It's the great things based in kindness and love that we do for others that sets us up for the great things based in kindness and love that others do for us. Just as your job helps you to meet certain needs in your life, you help your organization to complete certain needs it has with the time, talents and efforts you give to the company.

> *"Be not deceived, God is not mocked; for whatsoever a man soweth, that shall he also reap." ~ Galatians 6:7 (The Bible)*

Every aspect of your job matters. By tying together everything we've said so far, you can learn not to hate your job. When you <u>Understand It</u>, you'll grow to accept what your job does to help you in your life and it'll then help you to <u>Appreciate the Fact</u> that you even have a job. When you use your time and gifts properly, you'll <u>Make the Most</u> of your time while at work and grow to <u>Accept Your Value</u> and the impact that you play in helping to fulfill the purpose and mission of the company you work for. As a vital employee, <u>Avoid the Gossip</u> that some people participate in by making sure you <u>Don't Complain</u> about situations and circumstances that arise. When you <u>Know Your Importance</u> and understand that you help make your company successful because you took the time to <u>Find the Purpose</u> in what you do to help the organization, you'll consistently <u>Strive for Excellence</u> and <u>Make It</u>

About Others and the purpose of the company. As a mature and positive employee, you can Bring The Sunshine to others and the company when you Become Positively Noticeable to all those you work with understanding that Everything Matters.

> *"A gift - be it a present, a kind word or a job done with care and love - explains itself!... and if receivin' it embarrasses you, it's because your 'thanks box' is warped."* ~ Alice Childress

In everything you do, strive to have a positive impact on others and the mission of the company you work for. Expect the good to come to you in response to the good you do for others. Expect the good to come to you in response to the good you say to others. Expect the good to happen in your life in response to the good that you help to happen in the life of someone else. Expect the best on your job because you have given your job your best. You are important and what you do is important. So, keep in mind that everything you do matters towards the impact you have on others, the impact you have on your job and the impact your job has on you.

13 Viewpoints For Satisfaction At Work

MY BOSS IS A JERK

Jerk [jurk] noun – Slang. a contemptibly naive, fatuous, foolish, or inconsequential person.

Ok, let's say that all we said about what you need to do and how to adjust yourself makes perfect sense and you have made a decision to do all of the things that we've talked about so far. However, despite all of that you're left with, one true and disturbing thought that resonates in your head, which is, "My Boss is a Jerk!"

So, for those people who may be thinking or living through that, let's talk about it. Unfortunately, there may be times, during your working career, that you may need to submit to the authority of a jerk. However, it doesn't have to turn your job into a miserable place to be. So here are some simple thoughts to help you deal with a boss of "Jerk-ology."

> *"If you have a job without aggravations, you don't have a job." ~ Malcolm Forbes*

UNDERSTAND THE POSITION

position [puh-zish-uh n] noun – condition with reference to place; location; situation; a place occupied or to be occupied; situation or condition, especially with relation to favorable or unfavorable circumstances; status or standing:

Your boss will always have a different level of responsibility than you. Of course, this does not give them the right to be a jerk. Some people, quite frankly, don't know how to handle pressure, and it could be that the pressure of the position they hold is a bit too much for them. If so, you may get the short end of the stick when working with them. So, open up your heart and mind to trying to understand what your boss may be dealing with. Try to understand that their responsibilities are different from yours and their added responsibilities may add stress to their life that they may not handle well.

The position that they hold may come with stress that they have never learned how to properly manage. Take into account that there may be things in their position that help to create the negative behaviors you may see. This again, doesn't make it right, it's just a viewpoint or personal perspective that you can have so that you can relate to them a little better.

UNDERSTAND THE PERSON

Person [pur-suh n] noun – a human being, whether an adult or child; a human being as distinguished from an animal or a thing.

Some people enjoy lording their positions over others. People that feel this way enjoy acting like jerks to others because it increases their own sense of control. By understanding what this type of person needs to feel important, it'll help you to understand how they operate and make it easier for you to deal with their negative behaviors. These types of people are normally insecure, immature and probably feel inadequate about something within themselves.

The secret to this type of person is to simply know how to deal with them. If your boss demands unconditional compliance, give it to him freely as long as it does not cross the line into disrespect or dishonor for you. What we mean by that is, if they want to be updated minute by minute on everything you do, take it up a notch and update them second by second, and do it with a smile. We can almost guarantee that if you take what they are demanding and comply with their unreasonable request in a slightly overboard but pleasant manner, they will soon get tired of it and remove their previous requirement just to get you off their back.

Social and interpersonal skills aren't always taught at colleges and universities. So, your boss may have learned the skills required for the business of the company but have no clue on how to operate the business of people. Keep in mind that the position they hold in the company may have nothing to do with the position they hold with people in their personal life. They may have no idea how to honor people, so once you understand this, don't let their jerkiness bother you too much, if possible have a little compassion on them knowing that there's always a source to a person's behavior. Some people are a public success but a private failure. If you see negative behavior coming from a person, its normally a result of some type of negative situation in their life. So, strive to have compassion for these types of people and "Bring The Sunshine" to them as much as possible despite their jerkiness.

UNDERSTAND THE TIME

time [tahym] noun – duration regarded as belonging to the present life as distinct from the life to come or from eternity; finite duration; a system or method of measuring or reckoning the passage of time:

At the end of the day, no matter what goes on, what happens or what's said, the fact of the matter is, you get to go home at the end of the day. If you always see the light at the end of the tunnel while working with a jerk of a boss, grin and bear it knowing that it will pass whenever you get to go home. So, earn your money, do your job in excellence and go home. Then make sure you leave that jerk at work! Don't take him home with you!

The time you spend at work is for a specific purpose to advance your life. Even if you are working to move up in the company, know that your time with a jerk for a boss will not last forever. If you do your job well with a great attitude, you may be promoted above your jerk of a boss and then you can show them how a boss is supposed to treat others. So, understand the time that you have to spend with their jerkiness and find comfort in the fact that it will not last forever.

UNDERSTAND THE CONTROL

control [kuh n-trohl] verb – controlled, controlling; to exercise restraint or direction over; dominate; command; to hold in check; curb:

Always keep in mind that you have the control of your heart, mind and state of being. I learned something growing up that I try and govern my life by, and that is this, "There's never an excuse for a bad attitude." Now sometimes I've had to make hard decisions, to let go of friends or associates and say things that may have been hard to say. However, if my attitude was positive and uplifting, it always helped the situation be a little easier to face because of my own personal attitude. Being happy is a decision and state of mind which cannot be taken away, only given away.

One way to make sure that you aren't moved by a jerk of a boss is to not be surprised or upset when, "A Jerk Acts Like A Jerk." Acting like jerks is what jerks do, so why should that surprise you? The Bible says, in Luke 6:43 & 44, *"For a good tree does not bear bad fruit, nor does a bad tree bear good fruit. For every tree is known by its own fruit."* If you pay attention to this wisdom, you will know the fruit of a jerk of a boss and not let it surprise you. Know it, understand it and move on knowing that you remain in control of your life and emotions.

You are in control of your happiness if you decide to take control of it. If you let someone else steal your joy, blame yourself, not them. Understand that your jerk of a boss is not in control of your heart or your mind, and you can always overcome their evil with good. You have the control of how things affect you, so make sure they don't affect you the wrong way.

13 Viewpoints For Satisfaction At Work

AFTER WORK

af·ter [af-ter, ahf-] – preposition 1. behind in place or position; following behind: 2. later in time than; in succession to; at the close of:

One way to make it easier to cope with your hours at work is to make the most of your time away from work. Your job should be done to the best of your ability while you are there, but once you leave work, have some fun. Do something that makes you happy. Do something that does not remind you of your job.

The key thing to stress here is separation. You must separate your hours at work from your hours with your family, your hours having fun and your hours of enjoying other aspects of life. If you take your job home with you, then your work hours, in essence, haven't ended. It would then be no wonder why you hate going to your job, because your heart and mind never left.

Could it be that your job is really not that bad? Perhaps you have just been working nonstop for years and you just might need a real break from your job? When every aspect of your life has a specific place to reside, it's easier to maintain order and peace.

One day, when my mother was training me on how to keep my room clean, she taught me a very simple concept, which I would like to share with you. She said, "Find a place for everything in your room. Every toy, every comic book, your school books, your shoes, your clean clothes, your dirty clothes, your hamsters, your turtles and all your drawing pencils and stuff should have a specific place in your room. Now when you use them, just put them back where they belong. So if you're using a lot of things, when it's time to clean up, you know what to do, because everything has its place."

This same principle applies to every aspect of our lives. Everything has its place. There's a place for God, a place for your friends, a place for your mate, a place for your family and a place for your job. Some places are more important and protected than others, yet they all have a place. So when work is over....work is over. Switch your mind to another channel and breathe. It will make going back to work the next day easier to approach, easier to get through, and easier to handle.

"Don't be afraid to give your best to what seemingly are small jobs. Every time you conquer one it makes you that much stronger. If you do the little jobs well, the big ones tend to take care of themselves." ~ Dale Carnegie

PURSUE HAPPINESS

happiness [hap-ee-nis] noun – the quality or state of being happy. good fortune; pleasure; contentment; joy.

You may not have your dream job. Maybe you love to write poetry or work on cars. Maybe you love balloons and the smiles they put on children's faces when they get one. Take time to pursue those things that make you happy. There's a time to pursue money and a time to pursue a career, and then there's a time to pursue happiness. I believe that God loves us all and wants us to be happy and not just exist.

There is no such thing as the pursuit of happiness, but there is the discovery of joy. ~ Joyce Grenfell

He has given you something in life that you enjoy. Take time to find out what it is and like Nike says, "Just Do It." Don't do it for money at first, just do it because you like it. If you do it long enough, it can lead to that thing that you can do for money. First, find that thing that you do just because you like to do it. Find that happy place away from work to help bring peace and balance to your life.

If you find that thing that you can do for free and do it well enough, eventually someone may be willing to pay you for it. Having pleasure is NOT happiness. Pleasure is momentary while happiness is long lasting. So find something that just makes you happy and do it. It'll make going back to your job that much easier.

PURSUE PURPOSE

purpose [pur-puh s] noun – the reason for which something exists or is done, made, used, etc; an intended or desired result; end; aim; goal; practical result, effect, or advantage:

We consider purpose to be something that's only fully realized when it benefits someone else other than you. For example, a car can be modern, nice, comfortable and sporty, but its ultimate purpose is for its passengers to safely ride in. Food can be tasty and even filling, but the ultimate purpose for food should be to provide energy and nourishment to the body.

So, if you want to find true fulfillment in your life, search for a purpose that provides you with fulfillment and satisfaction by serving something of benefit to others. For example, baking cakes may provide fulfilment to a baker because of the purpose of providing cakes for people to celebrate birthdays, anniversaries and special events. Keep in mind that money does not make you happy, it's living a life of purpose that makes life worth living.

Take the time to find your passions and pursue the purpose in them. By doing so, you'll find enjoyment that your job may not bring. And if you do it well enough, you may be able to develop your pursuit of purpose into a fulfilling, successful and prosperous business.

"As long as people will accept crap, it will be financially profitable to dispense it."
~ Dick Cavett

THINGS TO CONSIDER

consider [kuh n-sid-er] verb – to think carefully about, especially in order to make a decision; contemplate; reflect on; to think, believe, or suppose; to bear in mind; make allowance for; to pay attention to; regard:

We've talked about a lot of things here but let's point out a few of them for further consideration. So please remember that:

- Many people are looking for jobs, so remember to be grateful for the one you have.
- As you strive to do your best on your job, you will feel a satisfaction and a sense of pride in what you do.
- No matter what goes on, become someone that the people around you enjoy working with. As they appreciate your presence and your work, you'll grow to appreciate them as well.
- Your job is part of your life; it's not your entire life, so find the balance.
- Find things that make you happy and make a conscious decision to separate yourself from

work. Spend time with other areas of importance in your life.

CLOSING

Thanks so much for joining us on this journey towards acceptance, appreciation and gratitude for your job. The mindset of not hating your job is available to everyone, but without a proper mindset shift, many people may never embrace it.

> *"Think enthusiastically about everything; but especially about your job. If you do, you'll put a touch of glory in your life. If you love your job with enthusiasm, you'll shake it to pieces. You'll love it into greatness." ~ Norman Vincent Peale*

It's important that you don't see your job as an awful part of your existence. Whether it's your dream job or not, it's a job and without it things could be a lot worse. Now, after you understand and accept that fact, adjust your viewpoint so that you can better appreciate your job and the people you work with. No one has the right to make your life miserable but you. Enjoy your life, thank God for your job and find purpose in the things you do.

Thanks again for reading! May success, happiness and fulfillment manifest in every area of your life and family!

BIBLIOGRAPHY

References Used:
- The Bible: King James and the Amplified Versions
- The Quotations Page – quotationspage.com
- Dictionary.com – dictionary.com
- Brainy Quotes – brainyquote.com

Endnotes:
- [1] Statista: The Statistics Portal - This text provides general information. Statista (content provider) assumes no liability for the information given being complete or correct. Due to varying update cycles, statistics can display more up-to-date data than referenced in the text.
  https://www.statista.com/topics/771/employment/
- [2] The National Center for Biotechnology Information
  https://www.ncbi.nlm.nih.gov/pubmed/9569648
- [3] Forbes Magazine Best Companies to Work For
  http://money.cnn.com/magazines/fortune/bestcompanies/2010/snapshots/4.html

13 Viewpoints For Satisfaction At Work

OTHER BOOKS

Below are a few books by Eric M. Watterson. You may find them listed on Amazon.com or by clicking the title. You may also find these titles and others listed online at: **CENTRY.me** under "CENTRY Curriculum". Thank You!

- Manhood 101: 101 Principles for Becoming a Better Man
- The Power of Touch: Your 14 Days Guide To A Stronger Relationship
- The Honor of Her: The Benefit of Honoring Her in Life & Relationship
- How Not 2 Hate Your Job: 13 Viewpoints for Satisfaction at Work
- How to Get Along with Everyone: Simple Keys for Success with Others
- Selfish or Selfless: Which One Are You?
- The Path of Forgiveness: How to Give & Receive Total Forgiveness
- I Forgive You: Why You Should Always Forgive
- I Just Can't! How to Forgive the Unforgiveable

- **Didn't You Forgive Me? How to Be Restored After Being Forgiven**
- **Your Strength As A Man**
- **DAD: Forgiving What He Was, Becoming What He Was Not**

FOLLOW US @

Facebook.com/**iamcentry**

Twitter.com/**iamcentry**

Instagram.com/iamcentry/

YouTube Channel "iamCENTRY"

13 Viewpoints For Satisfaction At Work

MORE INFO

SERVE · HONOR · PROTECT

For more information concerning the CENTRY™ Brand, along with additional books, courses, services, mentoring and offers intended to help guys Serve, Honor & Protect their wives, children, families, communities and the world, visit us online at:

"CENTRY.me" and "CENTRYLeague.com"

The CENTRY™ League "**Choose Greatness Personal Development & Mentoring Program**" consists of our series of workbooks and online courses that we use to mentor and coach males in 7 Specific Areas that will inspire, assist and lead them to Choose Greatness in their lives.

For more information visit:

ChooseGreatness.me